A Comprehensive Guide To Essential UK Criminal Law Cases

LUC JORGART

Copyright © 2020 Luc Jorgart

All rights reserved.

ISBN: 9798559018232

CONTENTS

1	Transferred Malice	Pg 1
2	The Chain of Causation	Pg 4
3	Intention	Pg 11
4	Third Parties	Pg 15
5	Duty of Care	Pg 18
6	Medical Incidents	Pg 20
7	The Queens Peace & War	Pg 22
8	Defences	Pg 24
9	What Amounts to a Crime ?	Pg 33
10	Other Cases	Pg 41

1 TRANSFERRED MALICE

R v Latimer (1886)
Facts of the case: Two men got into a fight at a bar (the defendant being one of them). The defendant took off his belt and went to hit the other man. He missed and hit a woman instead.

Principle: The fact that the defendant had intended to hit the man and not the woman is irrelevant. If you intend to cause harm, then that intent can be transferred to the victim.

Quick memory: R v Latimer - belt slap - transferred malice

R v Mitchell (1983)
Facts of the case: The defendant cut in line inside of a post office. An elderly man took issue with the action and challenged the defendant. The defendant pushed the elderly man who subsequently fell onto an elderly woman who died from the incident. The defendant was convicted of manslaughter.

Principle: There is no legal requirement that an unlawful act must be directed at the victim.

Quick Memory: R v Mitchell (1983) - pushed man who fell into another - transferred malice

R v Saunders (1573)

Facts of the case: The defendant wanted to kill his wife so that he could marry another woman. The defendant poisoned an apple and gave it to his wife. His wife gave the apple to their daughter who subsequently died.

Principle: An intention to kill someone will be passed to the victim regardless of who you intended to kill.

Quick memory: R v Saunders - poison apple given to wife who gave to daughter - transferred malice

R v Gnango (2012)

Facts of the case: The defendant was a drug dealer and carrying a firearm went looking for a man named TC. Gnago could not find TC so decided to wait in his car when he saw a man in a red bandana walking towards him with a firearm. The red bandana man (suspected to be TC) began opening fire and a shootout between the 2 continued. An unsuspecting care worker was caught in the crossfire and shot dead. Despite the fact it was proven that it was the red bandana man's bullet that hit the care worker and that the red bandana man shot first, Gnango was convicted of murder.

Principle: If you create a dangerous situation you may be held accountable for the resulting actions.

Quick memory: R v Gnango - gangland shooting - transferred malice (creation of dangerous situation)

R v Pembleton (1870)
Facts of the case: A man threw a rock into a crowd intending to hit someone but instead the rock smashed a window. The defendant was found not guilty of criminal damage.

Principle: Transferred malice cannot be applied between different crimes.

Quick memory: R v Pembleton - threw rock to hit someone but smashed window - transferred malice for different crimes (not guilty)

2 THE CHAIN OF CAUSATION

R v Pagett (1983)
Facts of the case: The defendant armed with a gun took a 16-year-old who was pregnant with his child hostage. The defendant then used her as a human shield and fired shots at police. The police fired back and the girl was shot by the police and later died.

Principle: If you cause events that would most certainly cause foreseeable events then you are guilty of the events which transpire.

Quick memory: R v Pagett - pregnant girlfriend used as shield - chain of causation

R v Thao-Meli (1954)
Facts of the case: There were 4 men convicted of murder. They had planned to get someone drunk, hit them over the head and make their death look like an accident. They hit the man over the head and believing he was dead they took his body to a cliff and threw him off of it. Medical evidence showed that he did not die from the strike to the cliff but instead survived and died from the natural elements at the bottom of the cliff. The defendants argued that they did not have an actus reus (guilty act) while having a mens rea (guilty mind) as they had believed he was dead when they threw him off the cliff. However, the court ruled it was all the same act.

Principle: In murder, the act of killing someone is a continuing act.

Quick memory: R v Thao-Meli - actus reus and mens rea separation - continuing act

R v Hughes (2013)
Facts of the case: The victim had taken heroin and went driving. The defendant had no insurance but was not drunk or driving in a way that is reckless. The victim and defendant crashed causing the victim to die. It was proven there was no way the defendant could have prevented the crash. The court said that if the man was to crash into a tree and die would the blame be on the man who planted the tree.

Principle: The defendant must cause a culpable act to be guilty.

Quick memory: R v Hughes - crashed with heroin driver who died but Hughes had no insurance - chain of causation

R v Malcherek and Steel (1981)
Facts of the case: These were two similar appeals which were heard together. In both cases women were beaten and taken to hospital where they were put on life support. In both cases the doctors turned off life support. The defendants argued that turning of the life support was an intervening act which broke the chain of causation. This appeal was unsuccessful.

Principle: Life support being turned off is not an intervening act unless it is turned off negligently.

Quick memory: R v Malcherek and Steel - life support - medical chain of causation

R v Cheshire (1991)

Facts of the case: The defendant shot a man in a chip shop. The victim had to have surgery and in several weeks his wounds were healed however he continued to have difficulty breathing and later died from complications from the surgery. The defendant was convicted of murder and appealed.

Principle: Intervening medical treatment can only exclude the responsibility of death if it was so independent and potent that the defendants act is seen as insignificant.

Quick memory: R v Cheshire - chip shop shooting - medical chain of causation

R v Smith (1959)

Facts of the case: The defendant was a soldier in the army. He got into a fight with a fellow soldier and stabbed him with a bayonet. On the way to receive treatment the victim was dropped on the stretcher twice by the medics. Then once the victim had arrived, there was an error in communication and the doctors were under the impression he was just scratched. The soldier later died and Smith was charged but argued that if the soldier had received proper medical care he would not have died.

Principle: If the injury was the active cause of death then the conviction will be upheld.

Quick memory: R v Smith (1959) - barracks room fight - medical chain of causation

R v Roberts (1971)
Facts of the case: After a party Roberts offered the victim a ride to another party. During the car journey Roberts kept making unwanted sexual advances towards the victim despite her rejecting his advances. She then jumped out of the moving vehicle and got injured as a result. Roberts was convicted of sexual assault and actual bodily harm.

Principle: If your actions cause the victims actions then you hold the blame.

Quick memory: R v Roberts - girl jumped out car after rob touching her - chain of causation

R v Blaue (1975)
Facts of the case: The defendant stabbed a girl four times. She was a religious Jehovah's Witness and so refused a blood transfusion which would save her life. The defendant was convicted of manslaughter and appealed.

Principle: A victim's refusal of medical care does not break the chain of causation. You must take your victims as you find them (the thin skull rule).

Quick memory: R v Blaue - Jehovah witness - must take your victim as you find them

R v Haywood (1908)
Facts of the case: The defendant chased the victim out of his house while shouting at her. She collapsed and died due to a medical condition which both parties were unaware of. However, there was no physical contact. The defendant was found guilty of manslaughter.

Principle: It is not relevant if your actions would cause a normal person to die. You must take your victims as you find them.

Quick memory: R v Haywood - defendant chased victim who died of fright due to medical condition - must take victims as you find them (not relevant whether normal person would die)

R v Hart (1986)
Facts of the case: The defendant assaulted the victim on a beach and left her unconscious. He left her below the high-water mark and she later drowned.

Principle: Ordinary events of nature do not break the chain of causation.

Quick memory: R v Hart - beat girl up who later drowned from high tide - chain of causation not broken by ordinary factor

R v Jordan (1956)

Facts of the case: The defendant stabbed the victim. The victim was taken to hospital where he was given medication despite showing an allergic reaction and later given excessive amounts of intravenous liquids. He died 8 days after admission due to pneumonia and at the time of death, his wounds were starting to heal.

Principle: If the medical treatment is so grossly negligent that it becomes the active cause of death the chain of causation is broken.

Quick memory: R v Jordan - victims stab wounds healed but died from reaction to too much medication - medical chain of causation broken

R v Kennedy (2007)

Facts of the case: The defendant filled a syringe with heroin and gave it to his friend who injected himself and died. The defendant was charged with manslaughter but appealed. It was said the victims' choice to inject heroin was voluntary.

Principle: When a victim makes a choice with a voluntary and informed decision, the chain of causation is broken.

Quick memory: R v Kennedy - supplied heroin to friend who died - chain of causation broken as he had a choice

R v Cato (1976)
Facts of the case: Cato and the victim were both heroin addicts who injected each other with heroin. The victim died and Cato was convicted of manslaughter.

Principle: Administering a noxious substance to another person (even if it's their choice) does not break the chain of causation.

Quick memory: R v Cato - Case where 2 addicts injected each other - chain of causation not broken

R v Glenn Paul Wright (2000)
Facts of the case: An inmate tied a makeshift noose to the ceiling of his cell and encouraged his cellmate (the victim) to hang himself and threatened the victim with violence if he refused.

Principle: If you encourage a suicide then you may be responsible for the actions which come after.

Quick memory: R v Glenn Paul Wright - inmate commands other inmate to hang himself – preparing and encouraging suicide constitutes murder

3 INTENTION

R v Woollin (1999)
Facts of the case: Woollin was alone with a baby and began shaking it when it started crying. Then the baby began choking and Woollin threw the 3-month old baby to the ground. The baby later died from the resulting injuries.

Principle: The defendant must have a virtual certainty that their actions will cause serious bodily harm to be guilty of murder.

Quick memory: R v Woollin - baby killed - no mens rea, state of mind during crime

R v Shivpuri (1986)
Facts of the case: The defendant was persuaded to smuggle drugs into the UK. He smuggled a suitcase which he believed to contain heroin or cannabis. When caught, he admitted to the crime but it then turned out the substance was legal vegetable powder.

Principle: You can't commit a crime that hasn't actually been committed.

Quick memory: R v Shivpuri - drug smuggler admitted crime but it was vegetable powder - can't commit for a crime that wasn't committed

R v Savage (1991)
Facts of the case: The defendant had a dislike towards her ex's new girlfriend (the victim). The defendant decided to throw a pint of beer at the victim in order to humiliate her. However, the defendant's beer glass fell out of her hand and cut the victims wrist.

Principle: For the offence of grievous bodily harm, the defendant does not have to have the intent to harm someone to be found guilty.

Quick memory: R v Savage - threw beer glass by accident instead of just beer - GBH does not require intent

R v Vickers (1957)
Facts of the case: The defendant broke into a shop premises in order to steal money. During the robbery, the defendant came across the victim who lived in the flat above the premises. The defendant attacked the victim and left. The victim later died of her injuries.

Principle: It does not matter if you intend to kill the victim. If you intend to commit GBH then you already have the mens rea for murder.

Quick memory: R v Vickers - broke into store and attacked victim - intent to commit GBH constitutes mens rea for murder

R v Bundy (1977)

Facts of the case: The defendant was following a parking meter collector with the alleged intent to rob her. Inside of the defendant's vehicle they found a hammer, a piece of piping and some pieces of stocking. He was charged with conspiracy to rob. However, the defendant argued that because he was homeless, his car was his place of abode.

Principle: A car is not a place of abode when it is in motion. However, when stationary it can be considered a place of abode.

Quick memory: R v Bundy - place of abode as car - going equipped for a crime

Jaggard v Dickinson (1981)

Facts of the case: The defendant was out drinking and became stranded so went to her friend's house. The friend had previously instructed the defendant to treat his house as her own. The defendant knocked on the door but there was no answer so the defendant smashed a window and broke into the house. It turned out the house did not belong to the defendant's friend but was instead a similar looking house. The defendant was originally convicted but appealed and had her conviction overturned.

Principle: The court must consider the belief of the defendant as well as their feelings.

Quick memory: Jaggard v Dickinson - broke into house while drunk - consider defendant's feelings

R v Williams (1983)
Facts of the case: The defendant saw a youth being dragged down the street by the victim while the youth was screaming for help. The defendant ran over to help the youth and a fight broke out. It turned out that the victim had seen the youth mug someone and reprimanded him.

Principle: A reasonable mistake can constitute a valid defence.

Quick memory: R v Williams - attacked a thief's attacker - mistake of facts

R v Lamb (1967)
Facts of the case: Two boys were playing with a revolver. There was a bullet in the gun but it was not in any of the chambers opposite the barrel which the boys believed meant it would not fire. The defendant pointed the gun at the victim and fired and killed the victim.

Principle: There can be no unlawful act if the defendant does not apprehend immediate physical violence.

Quick memory: R v Lamb - shooting friend - mistake

4 THIRD PARTIES

R v Betts and Ridley (1930)
Facts of the case: Two men agreed to rob a man and steal his bag. Betts would commit the robbery while Ridley would wait around the corner in a getaway car. When the robbery took place, Betts struck the victim with so much force that he died.

Principle: It is not necessary for an accessory of a crime to be present during the crime to be found guilty.

Quick memory: R v Betts and Ridley - mugger killed person - accessory presence

R v Jogee (2016)
Facts of the case: The defendant and his friend Hirsi spent a night drinking and becoming increasingly aggressive. Twice during the night, they visited Mrs. Reid who was in a relationship with the victim. After the second visit Reid had text the defendant saying not to bring Hirsi back to the house. The defendant and Hirsi returned. The victim had a verbal dispute with the two men. The defendant shouted encouragement to Hirsi (unaware that Hirsi was concealing a knife) and a fight broke out where Hirsi stabbed the victim who later died.

Principle: If you encourage someone to commit a crime then you can be found guilty of their actions under joint enterprise.

Quick memory: R v Jogee - encouraging violence - third party / joint enterprise

DPP for Northern Ireland v Lynch (1975)
Facts of the case: The defendant was ordered by a member of the IRA to drive a car. One of the men in the car called Meehan was known to the defendant due to Meehan's reputation of violence. The defendant was certain he would be shot if he did not comply. The three IRA members got out of the car and then shot and killed a policeman.

Principle: The graver the crime committed, the more serious the threat must be for the defendant (for the defence of duress).

Quick memory: DPP for Northern Ireland v Lynch - Man drives IRA to site of murder - the graver the crime under duress the more serious the threat must be for the defendant

R v Mitchell (2008)
Facts of the case: The defendant and some friends got into a fight by a taxi. One of the friends ended up killing another. The defendant was involved in the fight and was said by witnesses to have been aggressive and violent. She left but came back to get her shoes while the murder took place. She was not encouraging anyone to fight upon return. She was still found guilty under joint enterprise.

Principle: You are automatically a party to a crime under joint enterprise unless you communicate withdrawal.

Quick memory: R v Mitchell (2008) - Woman in fight lost shoes and was looking while murder occurred - If you don't communicate withdrawal, your involved in the joint enterprise.

R v Howe (1987)

Facts of the case: The defendant was commanded by another man to torture and kill the victim under the threat that he would succumb to a similar fate if he disobeyed. They ended up killing a second time.

Principle: Duress is not an acceptable defence for first degree murder. It does not matter if you or your family are threatened.

Quick memory: R v Howe - Bathroom killer - murder under duress

5 DUTY OF CARE

R v Miller (1983)
Facts of the case: The defendant was a squatter who fell asleep with a lit cigarette in his hands. He awoke to see the cigarette had started a small fire. He then went to another room and went back to sleep. He was charged with criminal damage.

Principle: If you create a dangerous situation then you have a duty to deal with the situation.

Quick memory: R v Miller - vagrant cigarette - duty to act after dangerous situation creation

R v Evans (2009)
Facts of the case: The defendant bought some heroin and gave it to his sister. The sister injected the heroin and had an overdose. The defendant recognised that his sister was having symptoms of an overdose. The defendant and his mother decided to not seek medical assistance as they were afraid of getting into trouble. They were convicted of gross negligence manslaughter.

Principle: You have a duty of care if you create a dangerous situation.

Quick memory: R v Evans - gave sister heroin and didn't call ambulance when recognising OD - had duty to act

R v Dytham (1979)

Facts of the case: The defendant was a police officer. He saw a man being kicked outside a nightclub and decided to leave him. The man was kicked to death. He was charged with misconduct in a public office.

Principle: If you're a civil servant then you always have a duty of care.

Quick memory: R v Dytham - police officer let victim get attacked - duty of care civil servant

6 MEDICAL INCIDENTS

Airedale NHS trust v Bland (1993)
Facts of the case: Bland was a victim of the Hillsborough disaster. Bland was kept alive by life support machines in a vegetative state but his brain stem was still functioning. The hospital wanted to turn off the life support as there was no way Bland would recover.

Principle: It is not unlawful to remove artificial life support unless it is done so negligently.

Quick memory: Airedale NHS trust v Bland - not unlawful to remove life support

RE A (2001)
Facts of the case: Two conjoined twins were joined at the pelvis. One was capable of surviving independently but the other was not. Medical evidence showed that if they remained together, they would both die. The parents refused to consent to an operation which would separate them. The doctors appealed to the courts and were allowed to continue with the operation.

Principle: Incident medical murder is not a criminal offence.

Quick memory: RE A - conjoined twins - incident medical murder not a crime.

R v Adomako (1994)

Facts of the case: Adomako was an anaesthetist for an eye operation. During the operation, the oxygen pipe became disconnected which should have been easily noticed and the patient died of a cardiac arrest. Adomako didn't notice this and was convicted of gross negligence manslaughter.

Principle: Gross negligent manslaughter requires a duty of care where a breach causing the death is serious enough to be a crime.

Quick memory: R v Adomako - anaesthetist - gross negligence manslaughter

7 THE QUEENS PEACE & WAR

R v Page (1954)
Facts of the case: The defendant was a British soldier who shot an Egyptian rebel while abroad. Page was found guilty of murder. The defendant argued that because the victim was not British, he was not under the queen's peace.

Principle: The victim does not have to be British to be under the queen's peace.

Quick memory: R v Page - rebel shot in war - queen's peace

R v Clegg (1995)
Facts of the case: The defendant was a soldier in Northern Ireland. The defendant was tasked with guarding a checkpoint. A vehicle approached the checkpoint but continued past the checkpoint without stopping. The defendant ordered the driver to stop but the driver continued so the defendant fired shots at the vehicle, killing one of the passengers. The defendant was convicted of murder.

Principle: Excessive force in war makes killings unlawful.

Quick memory: R v Clegg - soldier shooting car - excessive force

R v Adebolajo (2014)

Facts of the case: The defendant killed a member of the armed forces in a brutal manner. The defendant argued he was a soldier of Islam and was in a war with the British government and as such was not under the queen's peace.

Principle: The queen's peace is not a personal belief.

Quick memory: R v Adebolajo - soldier murder - queen's peace not personal belief

8 DEFENSES

R v Franklin (1883)
Facts of the case: The defendant took a large box and threw it over Brighton pier. The box hit a swimmer on the head and the swimmer died as a result.

Principle: The unlawful act committed must be a criminal offence, it is not sufficient if it is only against civil law.

Quick memory: R v Franklin - threw a box over the pier and killed - civil wrong can't be used in criminal court

R v Lipman (1970)
Facts of the case: The defendant had taken LSD. He was hallucinating and thought the girl he was in bed with was a snake and that he was falling to hell. He then crammed a bedsheet down her throat, killing her.

Principle: If you know the drugs are dangerous and risk serious harm to yourself or others then taking them are grossly negligent and reckless.

Quick memory: R v Lipman - thought girl was snake on LSD and killed - defence of intoxication

Attorney General for Northern Ireland v Gallagher (1963)

Facts of the case: Gallagher was frequently violent towards his wife especially when he drank alcohol. He bought some whiskey and a knife. He knew the whiskey would make him aggressive enough to kill his wife. He ended up killing his wife after drinking.

Principle: Dutch courage is not an excuse for murder as the was an intent to commit the crime beforehand.

Quick memory: Attorney General for Northern Ireland v Gallagher - drinks for Dutch courage to kill wife - Dutch courage is not an excuse

R v Tom Dudley and Edwin Stephens (1884)

Facts of the case: A ship became shipwrecked and the two defendants along with a cabin boy were stranded in an emergency boat. The defendants ran out of food and killed the cabin boy in order to cannibalize him. They claimed the murder was necessary to survive.

Principle: There is no excuse of necessity for a murder charge.

Quick memory: R v Tom Dudley and Edwin Stephens - kill cabin boy - no necessity for murder

R v Taylor (2002)
Facts of the case: The defendant had agreed to import class B drugs into the UK but he was given class A drugs instead. The court stated the defendant had not agreed to the crime.

Principle: An agreement must be specific when charged with a conspiracy charge.

Quick memory: R v Taylor - Smuggler agreed to import Class B but Class A was imported - defendant (accomplice) had not agreed to crime

R v Jones (1987)
Facts of the case: The defendants were schoolboys which were convicted of causing GBH after throwing their friend in the air with the intention of catching them. However, they missed and ruptured the spleen of their friend. Evidence had shown they had done this before and that all the kids had taken it as a joke with no intent to harm.

Principle: Consensual rough horseplay is a defence.

Quick memory: R v Jones (1987) - schoolboy dropped in frequent game - Consent to rough horseplay is a defence

R v Sharp (1987)

Facts of the case: Sharp joined a gang which carried out armed robberies. He noticed they all had guns and wished to leave. The gang threatened him with violence if he left so he joined the robbery. Someone was shot during the robbery and sharp was convicted of murder.

Principle: If you join a violent gang voluntarily then you can no longer plead the defence of duress.

Quick memory: R v Sharp - wanted to leave robbery when saw guns but threatened - If you voluntarily join a violent gang you lose excuse of duress

Haughton v Smith (1973)

Facts of the case: A van carrying stolen goods was stopped by the police who allowed the van to continue its route in order to catch the people who were receiving them. The defendant argued that since the police had stopped the van, the police had seized the goods. Therefore, they were no longer stolen goods meaning that no crime was committed.

Principle: You cannot commit an impossible crime.

Quick memory: Haughton v Smith - police seize van but let continue - impossible crime

R v Clinton (2012)
Facts of the case: Clinton and his wife both suffered from depression. They both agreed to take a break. Clinton became obsessed and began looking at suicide websites. She then revealed that she was having an affair. He asked her to come over so they could explain to the kids that the marriage was over. However, the kids were not there and he was drunk when she arrived. His wife allegedly taunted him and described in graphic detail the sexual acts she performed with other men. Clinton then beat her with a wooden pole and strangled her to death.

Principle: Infidelity is not a qualifying trigger in regards to loss of control, however it may be taken into account.

Quick memory: R v Clinton - cheating wife killed - cheating not excuse for murder

R v Valderrama-Vega (1985)
Facts of the case: The defendant was a retired police officer who was broke. He was caught with a substantial amount of cocaine in his suitcase. The defendant claimed the mafia had threatened to reveal to everyone that he was gay if he refused to smuggle the suitcase.

Principle: A serious threat may justify a minor crime.

Quick memory: R v Valderrama-Vega - broke & secretly gay smuggler threatened by mafia - serious threat may justify minor crime under duress

R v Pommell (1995)
Facts of the case: The defendant was with a friend when the friend had shown he had a gun in his possession. The friend stated that he was going to use it "to do some damage". The defendant then took the gun from the friend and held onto it for safekeeping to give the police in the morning. The police found the gun in his house and arrested him. The defence of duress was not available because according to the courts he should have handed the gun in immediately.

Principle: The defence of duress is not available after the time of threat has elapsed.

Quick memory: R v Pommell - Man in possession of gun he took from murderous friend - no excuse of necessity or duress after time of threat has elapsed

Hibbert v McKiernan (1948)
Facts of the case: The defendant would collect lost golf balls on a golf course. He would then sell them. He did not have permission to be on the golf course or to collect the golf balls. He was caught stealing them and convicted of theft but appealed claiming that since he found the abandoned balls the rule of "finders' keepers" applied.

Principle: Finders keepers is not a valid defence in court.

Quick memory: Hibbert v McKiernan - golf ball thief - finders' keepers not valid

R v Humphreys (1995)
Facts of the case: The defendant had been brought up by an alcoholic mother and turned to prostitution at a young age. She moved in with an older man who was violent towards her. One day he tried to have intercourse with her and she refused so he mocked her self-harming scars. She responded to this by stabbing him. A doctor had concluded that she had attention seeking traits.

Principle: Attention seeking can be taken into account when assessing the defendant's standard of control.

Quick memory: R v Humphreys - attention seeker freed - attention seeking can help a defence

R v Steer (1988)
Facts of the case: Steer had an argument with a former business partner. Steer went around to the victims' house and rang the doorbell. He then proceeded to fire a gun through the door and windows of the property. His conviction was quashed as the danger to life came from the gun and not the property.

Principle: To convict someone of criminal damage, the prosecution must prove that the danger to life resulted from the actual destruction or damage to the property.

Quick memory: R v Steer - man shoots gun through window - danger to life must come from property for criminal damage

R v Bailey (1983)

Facts of the case: The defendant went to the house of his former lover's new boyfriend. The defendant was visibly upset and the victim (the new boyfriend) invited the defendant in for a cup of tea and to sort it out. The defendant was diabetic and told the victim he was not feeling well. He then asked the victim for water and sugar. Ten minutes later the victim bent over and the defendant struck the victim with an iron bar. The defendant claimed he committed the actions because he hadn't eaten.

Principle: Self-induced automatism (other than those induced by drugs and alcohol) may provide a defence to crimes of basic intent.

Quick memory: R v Bailey - diabetic smacks man with bar - Self-induced automatism may provide defence

Fardon v Harcourt-rivington (1932)

Facts of the case: The defendant and his wife left their dog in the car. The dog saw something exciting and pawed against the glass. The glass subsequently broke and a piece of glass flew into the plaintiff's eye.

Principle: You cannot be found guilty for fantastic probabilities which no reasonable person would foresee.

Quick memory: Fardon v Harcourt-rivington - dog in window - fantastic probability

R v Scarlett (1993)

Facts of the case: Scarlett had ejected a drunk customer from his pub. The customer fell, hit his head and subsequently died. Scarlett was convicted of manslaughter and appealed.

Principle: If you don't use excessive force then there is no unlawful act.

Quick memory: R v Scarlett - no excessive force is no murder - self defence

9 WHAT AMOUNTS TO A CRIME?

R v Brown (1993)
Facts of the case: A group of men engaged in consensual BDSM sexual acts over a period of years and recorded them. The police found the recordings and arrested the men on the charge of ABH.

Principle: Even if a victim consents to being harmed, you are still guilty of a violent offence.

Quick memory: R v Brown - BDSM - consensual harm is still harm

P v DPP (2012)
Facts of the case: The defendant snatched a lit cigarette out of the victim's hand and was charged with robbery but found not guilty.

Principle: There must be some kind of physical contact between the defendant and the victim in order for a robbery to occur.

Quick memory: P v DPP (2012) - stolen lit cigarette out hand - must be physical contact for robbery

R v Ireland (1998)
Facts of the case: The defendant made a series of calls to a woman over the course of three months. The defendant would not talk but would stay silent and breathe heavily down the line. He was convicted of assault.

Principle: Silence can amount to an assault and psychological harm can in some cases be considered bodily harm.

Quick memory: R v Ireland - silent phone calls - silent calls amounts to assault

R v Thomas (1985)
Facts of the case: There was an accusation from an eleven-year-old girl that the school caretaker touched the bottom of her skirt and lifted it twice, however there were no witnesses. There was another accusation that the caretaker touched the bottom of a twelve-year-old girl's skirt and rubbed it whilst she was in the library.

Principle: In some cases, touching an item of clothing may constitute battery.

Quick memory: R v Thomas - in some cases touching an item of clothing is battery

R v Robinson (1977)

Facts of the case: A woman owed the defendant £7. The defendant approached the woman's husband while brandishing a knife and took £5. He was convicted of robbery but the conviction was quashed as he was under the belief he was owed the money.

Principle: There is no theft if you have an honest belief you are entitled to the item.

Quick memory: R v Robinson - guy takes money owed by force with knife - no mens rea as was under belief he was entitled

R v Harvey (1981)

Facts of the case: Three defendants gave £20,000 to the victim for a consignment of cannabis. The consignments turned out to be worth nothing. The defendant then kidnapped the victim's wife and child and threatened to rape and kill them unless they got their money back.

Principle: When you threaten somebody with criminal action and know your threatening actions amount to a crime, you lose the defence of "honest belief."

Quick memory: R v Harvey - fake weed results in kidnapping - you lose defence of honest belief with criminal action

R v Morris (1983)
Facts of the case: The defendant switched the labels on two pork joints in the supermarket in order to get the more expensive one for a cheaper price. He was convicted of theft.

Principle: You don't have to escape with stolen items to be convicted of theft, you merely have to appropriate them.

Quick memory: R v Morris - swapped pork labels to buy cheaper - don't have to get away with items, just appropriate them for theft

Pitham V Hehl (1977)
Facts of the case: The defendant offered for sale an item of furniture which belonged to another person.

Principle: If you appropriate an item as your own then you are guilty of theft.

Quick memory: Pitham V Hehl - offered others furniture for sale - only owner has right to sell, appropriation is theft

DPP v Lavender (1994)

Facts of the case: The defendant took a door off a council property and replaced his girlfriend's council flat door with the door he had stolen.

Principle: If you treat a stolen item as your own to dispose of, then you have the intention to permanently deprive.

Quick memory: DPP v Lavender - stolen council house door for gf - disposal includes dealing with item as if it's your own

R v Lloyd (1985)

Facts of the case: The defendant worked at a cinema. He would sometimes take the films and copy them and then return them to the cinema. He was arrested but found not guilty of theft.

Principle: Borrowing an item is not theft unless you have the intention to return the item with the virtue taken from it.

Quick memory: R v Lloyd - Took film from cinema to bootleg and returned - borrowing is not theft unless intention to return without virtue

R v Hinks (2000)

Facts of the case: The defendant befriended an elderly man of low intelligence. The defendant coerced the man into withdrawing funds amounting to £60,000 over the course of seven months. The defendant was convicted of theft.

Principle: An appropriation can exist, even when the victim consents to the appropriation.

Quick memory: R v Hinks - defendant befriended man of low intelligence and gained money - there can be appropriation even if the victim consents

R v Jones (1990)

Facts of the case: The defendant had found out that his ex-girlfriend is dating someone. The defendant got hold of a sawn-off shotgun and climbed in the back of the new boyfriend's car. The defendant then pointed the shotgun at the boyfriend, however the boyfriend managed to grab the shotgun and throw it out of the car window.

Principle: You do not need to fire the trigger of a gun to be found guilty of attempted murder, you merely need to go equipped with the intent to commit murder.

Quick memory: R v Jones (1990) - tried to kill ex's new boyfriend but victim threw gun out window - if you intend to commit murder and go equipped it is attempted murder without firing of trigger

R v Whybrow (1951)
Facts of the case: The defendant wired up a soap dish in his bathroom in order to give his wife an electric shock. He was charged with attempted murder but appealed and found not guilty.

Principle: For the charge of attempted murder, you must intend to cause death, an intention to cause GBH can't constitute attempted murder.

Quick memory: R v Whybrow - For attempted murder you must intend to cause death, intent to cause GBH is not enough

R v Collins (1973)
Facts of the case: The defendant set up a ladder outside a young woman's window and climbed it in order to watch her sleep naked. The woman woke up and saw the defendant at the window. She invited him in for sex, thinking that it was her boyfriend. After they had sex, she realised it was not her boyfriend and called the police.

Principle: In order to be convicted of trespassing there must be a substantial entry.

Quick memory: R v Collins - man outside window victim thought was boyfriend - must be substantial entry to be a trespasser

R v Dume (1986)

Facts of the case: The defendant released his dog from the lead and commanded it to kill a man. The dog knocked over and bit the victim.

Principle: It is an assault to threaten to set an animal on somebody.

Quick memory: R v Dume - man sets dog on another - it is assault to threaten someone with a dog

R v Smith (2011)

Facts of the case: Smith had arranged to meet Jordan in order to buy heroin from him. When Jordan arrived, two other men, along with Smith jumped Jordan and stole his heroin. The three attackers were charged with robbery.

Principle: Unlawful property is still property and theft of illegal items is still a crime.

Quick memory: R v Smith (2011) - Case of heroin dealer who got jumped and called police - stolen illegal items are still theft

10 OTHER CASES

R v Ahluwalia (1992)
Facts of the case: The defendant was violently abused by her husband for years. After one night her husband went to bed and the defendant created makeshift napalm and burnt her husband alive.

Principle: In some cases, a "slowburn" reaction is a loss of control.

Quick memory: R v Ahluwalia - killed abusive husband - slowburn effect is loss of control

R v Smith (1974)
Facts of the case: The defendant was the tenant of a flat. With permission, he installed some wiring. When he was later given notice to leave the flat, the defendant ripped out the wires from the property. The defendant was charged with causing criminal damage.

Principle: If you install an item in a rented property then the item belongs to the landlord. Also an honest belief of ownership is not prosecutable.

Quick memory: R v Smith (1974) - Tenants taking wiring case - any items installed belong to landlord but honest belief of ownership is not prosecutable

R v Ibrams and Gregory (1982)
Facts of the case: Ibram had been constantly terrorised by John Monk. Ibrams girlfriend left him to start a relationship with Monk. However, Monk was extremely violent towards her causing her to leave him. Monk was later arrested and Ibrams girlfriend then resumed the relationship with Ibrams. On his release, Monk started visiting the couple using violence and later slept with Ibrams girlfriend. The police had been contacted by Ibram but did not take any action. Gregory, a friend of Ibram, witnessed the violence from Monk. Together Ibram and Gregory plotted to teach Monk a lesson. Ibrams girlfriend would invite Monk to their house, seduce Monk and then Ibrams and Gregory would burst in and beat him up. When this happened, the two men burst in and lost control eventually beating Monk to death.

Quick memory: R v Ibrams and Gregory - Mr monk bully - loss of control (old law)

(Note that the above case is old law, I have kept it in this book for the history)

Fagan v Metropolitan Police Commissioner (1969)

Facts of the case: The defendant was sitting in his car when a police officer approached the vehicle and told the defendant to move it. The defendant reversed his car onto the foot of the police officer. The police officer shouted at the defendant to move the car off his foot at which point the defendant began swearing at the officer and turned the car engine off, refusing to move the vehicle. The defendant was convicted of assaulting a police officer in the execution of his duty. It was agreed by the court that the assault took place when Fagan had noticed the car was on the foot of the officer and refused to act.

Principle: Refusal to cease commencing an illegal act after noticing it will constitute both the mens rea and actus reus of a crime.

Quick memory: Fagan v Metropolitan Police Commissioner - car on foot - failure to act

R v Cunningham (1957)

Facts of the case: The defendant ripped a gas meter from a property in order to steal the money in the meter. The defendant was not aware that this would cause the gas to leak. The gas subsequently escaped and leaked into a neighbouring property, killing the defendant's mother-in-law.

Principle: If someone foresees a risk and takes it, he is liable for the consequences.

Quick memory: R v Cunningham - gas meter stepmother - awareness of risk/ mens rea

R v Arobieke (1988)
Facts of the case: The defendant was at a train station looking to confront the victim. The victim was terrified of the defendant and in a bid to avoid him ran across the train tracks but touched a live wire. The victim then died.

Principle: You must commit an unlawful act to be guilty of a crime.

Quick memory: R v Arobieke - A looking for K, train tracks - Unlawful act must be done

R v Sutcliffe (2011)
Facts of the case: The defendant created a group on Facebook called "The Warrington Riots" and invited 400 contacts. Members of the public reported the page and it was taken down but 47 people confirmed their attendance before this was done. The defendant was found guilty of inciting a riot.

Principle: You can be convicted for inciting criminal behaviour through social networking.

Quick memory: R v Sutcliffe - Warrington riots Facebook page made and invited contacts - Guilty of inciting a riot

R v Siracusa (1989)
Facts of the case: The defendant conspired to import drugs. The court stated you are guilty of conspiracy in a crime if you intend to actively participate in the crime or if you intend to passively participate in the crime by failing to stop the unlawful activity.

Principle: You do not have to get involved in the important matters of the crime. If you have agreed that a crime should be committed, then you are guilty of conspiracy.

Quick memory: R v Siracusa - drug smugglers caught - court does not need to prove intent to take part, you can be a silent partner in a conspiracy

R v Antoniuk (1995)
Facts of the case: The defendant was drinking and her lover (the victim) found her unconscious on the downstairs floor. The victim then dragged her up the stairs while her head was banging on all the steps. The victim then took her to bed and raped her. The defendant then went to the kitchen and returned with a knife and stabbed her lover.

Principle: External factors such as shock are capable of causing automatism.

Quick memory: R v Antoniuk - victim taken to bed and raped then got up and stabbed man - external factors can cause automatism

R v Hussey (1924)
Facts of the case: The defendant was barricaded in his room while the landlady and her henchman tried to break down the door to unlawfully evict the defendant. The defendant grabbed his gun and fired through the door, wounding one of them. The defendant was charged and found not guilty.

Principle: It is lawful to defend yourself and your home from being unlawfully evicted.

Quick memory: R v Hussey - man being unlawfully evicted shoots through door - Its lawful for a man to defend his home from unlawful eviction

R v Davies (1975)
Facts of the case: The defendant's wife was having an affair. The defendant saw his wife's lover walking towards her place of work and killed her. The court held that the lover walking towards the wife's place of work was a provocative act.

Principle: A provocative act does not need to be deliberately aimed at provoking the victim or come from the victim.

Quick memory: R v Davies - killed wife after seeing lover walking towards her work - A provocative act does not need to be aimed at the victim

R v Goodfellow (1986)
Facts of the case: Goodfellow was being harassed by two men and wished to move from his council property to another. In an attempt to get rehoused, he had set fire to his property to make it look like it had been petrol bombed. However, he was not aware that his wife and son were in the property, all of which died in the fire.

Principle: It is not required that an unlawful act is directed at the victim or even a person.

Quick memory: R v Goodfellow - petrol bombed house - unlawful act can be directed at anyone

www.ingramcontent.com/pod-product-compliance
Lightning Source LLC
Chambersburg PA
CBHW070854220526
45466CB00005B/1999